Life in the
Stone Age

By Deborah Lock

Assistant Editor Prerna Grewal
Senior Art Editor Ann Cannings
Project Art Editor Rashika Kachroo
Art Editor Mohd Zishan
Jacket Coordinator Francesca Young
Jacket Designers Amy Keast, Suzena Sengupta
DTP Designers Nand Kishor Acharya, Anita Yadav
Picture Researcher Nishwan Rasool
Producer, Pre-Production Rob Dunn
Producer Niamh Tierney
Managing Editors Deborah Lock, Monica Saigal
Managing Art Editor Diane Peyton Jones
Deputy Managing Art Editor Ivy Sengupta
Art Director Martin Wilson
Publisher Sarah Larter
Publishing Director Sophie Mitchell

Reading Consultant Jacqueline Harris
Subject Consultant James Dilley

First published in Great Britain in 2018
by Dorling Kinderslely Limited
80 Strand, London, WC2R 0RL

Copyright © 2018 Dorling Kindersley Limited
A Penguin Random House Company
18 19 20 21 22 10 9 8 7 6 5 4 3 2 1
001–307847–Jan/2018

A CIP catalogue record for this book is available from the British Library.
ISBN: 978-0-2413-1593-4

Printed and bound in China.

The publisher would like to thank the following for their kind permission to reproduce their photographs:
(Key: a-above; b-below/bottom; c-centre; f-far; l-left; r-right; t-top)
1 123RF.com: Adrian Wojcik. **4–5 123RF.com:** Natalia Lukiyanova (background). **5 Dorling Kindersley:**
Royal Pavilion & Museums, Brighton & Hove (clb). **6–7 iStockphoto.com:** Kdgeisler (b). **12–13 123RF.com:**
uillermo Avello; Gleb Semenov (background). **14 123RF.com:** Raldi Somers (cl). **15 Dreamstime.com:**
Isselee (bl). **16 Dorling Kindersley:** Royal Pavilion & Museums, Brighton & Hove (c). **18–19 Dreamstime.com:**
Alanjeffery. **22 Dorling Kindersley:** Pitt Rivers Museum, University of Oxford (cr); Royal Pavilion & Museums,
Brighton & Hove (clb). **25 123RF.com:** Pixphoto. **26 123RF.com:** Kalcutta (c). **27 123RF.com:** PaylessImages (cr).
28 Klint Janulis: (clb). **29 Klint Janulis.** **32–33 123RF.com:** Rcaucino. **35 123RF.com:** Adrian Wojcik.
37 Getty Images: Universal History Archive. **38–39 iStockphoto.com:** Nicolamargaret. **40–41 123RF.com:** Arindam
Banerjee (background). **Dorling Kindersley:** Dan Crisp (all). **42–43 123RF.com:** Дмитрий Гооль (Dmitry Gool).
44–45 123RF.com: jetfoto

Jacket images: *Front:* **123RF.com:** Arindam Banerjee; **Dorling Kindersley:** Royal Pavilion & Museums,
Brighton & Hove br, Science Museum, London cra

All other images © Dorling Kindersley
For further information see: www.dkimages.com

A WORLD OF IDEAS:
SEE ALL THERE IS TO KNOW

www.dk.com

Contents

The Stone Age

The Stone Age is the time
when the first people lived.

Old Stone Age
3.3 million–11,500
years ago

Flint hand axe

People made tools
for cutting meat.

Harpoon tips

People made new tools such as harpoon tips from deer antlers.

Middle Stone Age 11,500–6,500 years ago

New Stone Age 6,500–4,000 years ago

Polished axe head

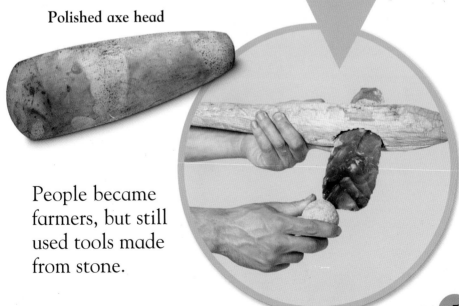

People became farmers, but still used tools made from stone.

Chapter 1
Setting up camp

Ice covered large parts of the
world at times in the Stone Age.
Early people had to find ways
to survive the cold.

People moved camps each season. They had to gather plants and hunt animals to eat and make tools. They followed the animals so that they could hunt them.

Animals such as deer moved from place to place to find food.

Stone Age
shelter

People needed good shelters to live in. The frames were made from thin tree branches. These were covered in animal skins, grass or tree bark. This kept the inside of the shelters warm and dry.

Animal skins covered the floor to keep the inside snug.

People wore clothes to keep warm. Deerskin was softened to make leather. Tunics and trousers were made from leather or plants.

Fur tunics were worn for hunting in winter. Fur shoes were filled with grasses for extra warmth.

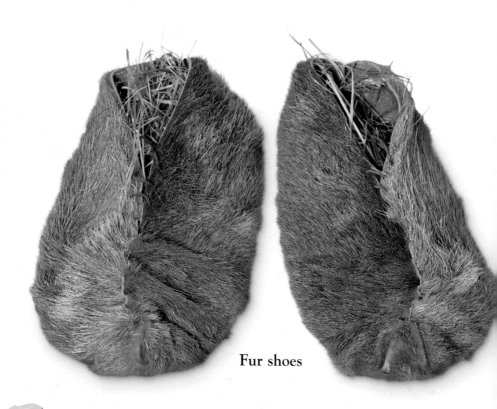

Fur shoes

Stone Age house

This New Stone Age
house had a grass roof.
Let's look inside.

Skara Brae,
Orkney Islands, UK

1

Chapter 2
On the hunt

Early people hunted all sorts of animals. They caught fish and other animals in rivers. They trapped birds.

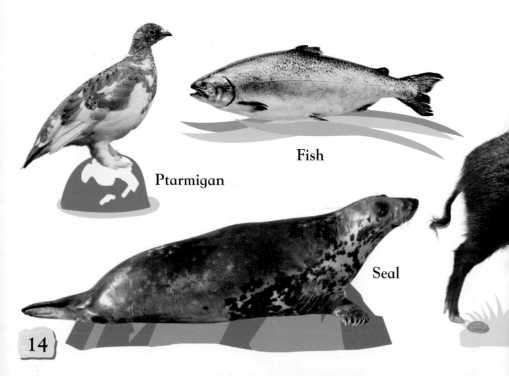

Fish

Ptarmigan

Seal

They hunted small animals like frogs and hares. There were also wild horses, wild boars and deer to hunt.

Frog

Brown hare

Deer

Wild boar

People needed good tools to catch the animals. They made tools out of wood, stone, bone, antlers and shells. The tools had sharp points to cut through the animal skin.

A fishing spear is also known as a harpoon.

Hunters waded in rivers to spear fish.

Stone Age people went hunting with dogs. They fed and tamed wolf cubs. These became the first dogs.

These tamed wolves also guarded the camps. They kept away dangerous wild animals like bears.

The large land animals like mammoths were dangerous to hunt. Stone Age hunters were brave. They learnt to throw long spears very fast and very far.

Spears were made from wood with stone or antler tips.

Every part of an animal was used – tusks and bones for tools, fur skin for clothes and the meat was eaten.

Stone Age tools

Stone Age people made tools for different jobs. They used tools to hunt, cut trees down and chop meat.

Hand axes were used to cut meat.

A pebble hammer helped to make axe blades.

People used flint blades to cut plants.

People hunted and fished using a spear.

Stone

A digging stick was used to plant crops.

Wood

Axes were used to cut trees down.

Chapter 3
Into the forest

Stone Age people did not just eat meat. They gathered plants such as fruits, nuts and roots.

Blackberries

Radishes

Hazelnuts

People knew which plants were good and which ones made them sick.

Greater burdock has a prickly flower head.

People also used plants for medicines. Some roots and leaves kept them healthy. They soaked burdock roots in hot water to make warm drinks.

Nettle leaves

Willow bark

Burdock roots

They added nettle leaves to soups. The bark of a willow helped to stop pain.

People used bark from trees to make buckets. They used these buckets to carry and store food and water. They wove flexible branches into baskets to trap fish.

Tree bark containers

Fish-catching basket

They wove long grass into roofs.
Rainwater ran down the outside
to keep the inside dry.

Wooden ladder

Making fire

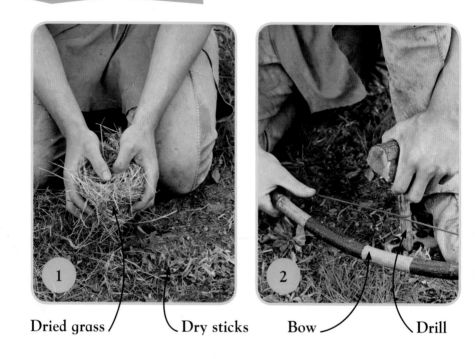

Dried grass / ⌐ Dry sticks

Bow ⌐ ⌐ Drill

Smoke ⌐

Small flames ⌐

Early people learnt how to make fire. Small dry sticks, dried grass and a bow drill were used.

They used the fire to cook food and keep warm. Fire also gave them light to work in the evening. Wild animals were scared of fire and stayed away.

Fire pit

Making rope

Early people made
rope from thin,
strong plant stems.
They used the rope
to make traps
and sew clothes.

Nettle
leaves
sting

You will need:
nettle plant

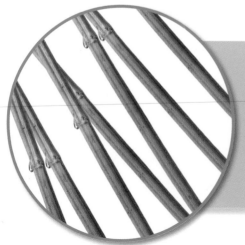

1. Strip the
leaves from
the stem.

2. Crush the stem with a thumb to soften it.

3. Strip away the outer layer and leave to dry.

4. Twist some outer layers together to make the rope.

Chapter 4
Celebrations

Early people used caves as shelters and as meeting places. They painted pictures on the walls. They used red, yellow and brown colours found in the soil. The black colour came from burnt wood, called charcoal.

Crushed red
rock in shell

Yellow
rock pebble

Charcoal

These hand paintings
are in Argentina.

Stone Age people believed in good and bad spirits. They drew the animals that they hunted on the cave walls. They may have been asking the animal spirits for good luck when hunting.

Shamans were people who led these rituals.

These cave paintings
are in France.

Some special places were marked with huge stones. These may have been meeting places for special days of the year.

Lots of people may have met together on the shortest day of the year. The stones at Stonehenge allow the setting sun to shine through.

Stonehenge is in the south of England, UK.

What came next?

People started to live in one place at the end of the Stone Age. They kept small farms to grow crops and raise animals.

Can you find these things in the picture:

 Pigs Cattle Farmer

 Sower 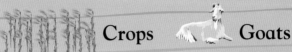 Crops 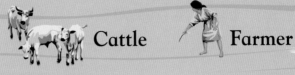 Goats

Quiz

1 In which part of the Stone Age did people become farmers?

2 What was leather made of?

3 What were used to make the frames for shelters?

4 Which animals became the first dogs?

5 Which tool was used to plant crops in the Stone Age?

6 Which leaves were added to soups in the Stone Age?

7 What did people in the Stone Age use to stop pain?

8 What was needed to make a fire in the Stone Age?

9 Who led the rituals?

10 What is charcoal?

Answers on page 45

Glossary

bark
hard outer covering of a tree

bow drill
small bow and a wooden drill used
to make fire in the Stone Age

crop
plants grown in large amounts

flint
hard stone used for tools in the
Stone Age

frame
firm, strong shape

harpoon
long spear with a pointed end

leather
material made from animal skin

mammoths
large animal with thick fur and
long curved tusks

medicine
something used to treat illness

ritual
ceremony with a set of actions

season
winter, spring, summer or autumn

shaman
person believed to have powers
to heal people and speak to spirits

shelters
covered place for people to live in
for a short time

sower
person who scatters seeds in a field

tunic
piece of knee-length clothing

Answers to the quiz:

1. New Stone Age; 2. Animal skin; 3. Thin branches;
4. Wolves; 5. Digging stick; 6. Nettle leaves; 7. Willow
bark; 8. Small dry sticks, dried grass and a bow drill;
9. Shamans; 10. Burnt wood

Guide for Parents

DK Readers is an exciting four-level reading series for children that will help to develop the habit of reading widely for both pleasure and information. These chapter books have an engaging main narrative to suit your child's reading ability, interspersed with additional information spreads in a range of reading genres. Each book is designed to develop your child's reading skills, fluency, grammar awareness and comprehension in order to build confidence and pleasure in reading.

Ready for a *Beginning to Read* book
YOUR CHILD SHOULD

- be using phonics, including consonant blends, such as br, sp and st, to sound out unfamiliar words; and be familiar with common word endings, such as plurals, ing, ed and ly.
- be using the meaning of the text, the grammar of a sentence plus clues from the illustrations to check and correct his/her own reading.
- be pausing briefly at commas, and for longer at full stops; and altering his/her expression for question, exclamation and speech marks.

A VALUABLE AND SHARED READING EXPERIENCE

For many children, reading requires a lot of effort, but adult participation can make this both fun and easier. So here are a few tips on how to use this book with your child.

TIP 1 **Check out the contents together before your child begins:**
- read the text about the book on the back cover.
- read through and discuss the contents page together to heighten your child's interest and expectation.
- have a brief discussion about unfamiliar or difficult words on each page.
- chat about the non-fiction reading features used in the book, such as headings, captions and labels.

TIP 2 Support your child as he/she reads each page:

- give the book to your child to read and turn the pages.

- where necessary, encourage your child to break a word into syllables, sound out each one and then flow the syllables together. Ask him/her to reread the sentence to check the meaning.

- you may need to help read some topic-related vocabulary and other words that may be difficult for your child.

- when there's a question mark or an exclamation mark, encourage your child to vary his/her voice as he/she reads the sentence. Demonstrate how to do this if it is helpful.

TIP 3 Praise, share and chat:

- the additional information spreads are designed to be shared and discussed with your child. These spreads tend to be more difficult than the main narrative.

- ask your child questions about the meaning of the text and of the words used. This will help to develop comprehension skills and awareness of the language used.

A FEW ADDITIONAL TIPS

- Encourage your child to try reading difficult words by themselves. Praise any self-corrections, for example, "I like the way you sounded out that word and then changed the way you said it to make sense."

- Try to read together every day. Reading little and often is best. These books are divided into manageable chapters for one reading session. However, after 10 minutes, only keep going if your child wants to read on.

- Read a variety of books of different types with your child for pleasure and information. Reading aloud to your child is a great way to develop his or her reading skills!

- Make reading an enjoyable experience for your child.

Index